MY HEART DANCES

LAURAINE J WAGNER

Mountain Ash
Press

INTRODUCTION

The granddaughter of Scandinavian pioneers, this remarkable woman was born Lauraine J. Johnson, 1926 in Holyoke, CO. You can feel the lonely high plains sky and the weight of the mountains in her writing.

Even into her eighties she would drive out from Ft. Collins to Pawnee Buttes for solace and inspiration.

Most of her poetry was written later in her life and with that perspective she gives equal value and love to the people, events and natural world that influenced her creativity.

After graduating high school at 16 and playing on the boys' sports teams, she earned a degree in journalism from DU. All four of her sons could read before starting school and she taught them all how to play sports. (She was Denver City Park horseshoes champ as a youth.)

Her husband Rick's 22-year career in the Air Force took them across the US and Europe. Throughout their travels and raising a family Lauraine studied different arts and crafts. A selection of her pen and ink drawings are included here.

After the Air Force they moved to Annapolis, MD and an editor's job at the Evening Capital where she rose to department head and mentored young journalists.

Laraine's life was a lesson in living by example. Her poems demand the same honesty and integrity of the reader. Her rich inner life of love, loss, sorrow, and reverence is revealed through her words.

PART ONE

This is the day we were made for.
Here is the place we belong,
This is the way we were meant to love,
Here is where we sing our song.

MY HOME TOWN

We left my home town over 80 years ago and never lived there again. But some of my favorite and most vivid memories are from there.

The first snow of winter always reminds me of the huge snowstorm that buried our town when I was six years old. The prairie wind drove the snow against one side of the bank building and packed it so hard that we could climb to the top of the bank and sled down. What a treat since there are no hills anywhere around.

That little town is Paoli, Colorado. It lies a couple of hours east of Fort Collins on Rt. 6 equally between Haxtun and Holyoke.

We happened to live there because my grandparents homesteaded near Holyoke in the mid 1800s and all their children were born in Holyoke, including my father. So I, too, was born in Holyoke, but we lived just 8 miles away in Paoli because my Dad managed the bank there.

It was a typical farm center on the prairie where farmers brought their harvest to the grain elevators to be shipped on the Burlington Northern Railroad, to get loans and make deposits at the bank.

There was a two-room schoolhouse, the first six grades were in one room and high school in the other. We had a small grocery store and a combined poolroom and bar where my dad used to take me (to my mother's dismay), and set me on the bar with a soft drink to watch the men shoot pool. That was it: no church, no restaurant, no stores. But all those things were just 8 miles away in either direction. We drove to Holyoke for church, shopping and to visit family.

We had to be creative to pass the summer days. Sliding down our cellar doors was one skill we worked at... Yes, just like that old song... Once, while sliding down standing up and backwards I slipped and fell on my hands puncturing one through the palm. And we did "holler down rain barrels" trying to create scary echoes.

I made up a game once that entertained the neighbor kids for a while. We would hold an egg while swinging and try to drop it onto a target on the ground. We were just getting good at it when Mother noticed the eggs were gone.

One day Dad took me to Holyoke and we got to ride in Dr. Jones' airplane. He flew low over Paoli so we could wave out the window to my mother who was hanging laundry on the clothesline. She was shocked and scolded dad severely for risking my life! What a thrill!

I remember having my tonsils taken out at the Haxtun hospital. I was there for three days for recovery, no complications, and loved all the ice cream they gave me and having everyone come visit.

Sundays we went to church in Holyoke where my aunt, uncle and three cousins lived. Then to their big house for dinner. My two older cousins like to play school with me as their student. They had me reading and writing, adding and subtracting before I ever entered school so I moved from the first grade row to the third grade row very quickly.

I'll never forget the night I went to the outhouse alone with a flashlight. I laid it on the bench and, before I could sit down, it rolled down the hole! The town entertainment for the next three days was to look down the hole to see if the light was still on.

Of course, every child was taught the lifesaving tornado lesson: lie down in the ditch, face down, and don't look up! I never had to do it. However, a tornado destroyed my grandparents' place in 1907. Everyone survived by going into the root cellar. I have the slightly battered family bible which also survived.

In 1933, after FDR closed the banks, we moved to Denver and into a new world. My first memory there, when we were in a hotel on 16th Street, is the sound of the trolly cars passing and the smell of maple syrup from the restaurant below. Things I would never experience in Paoli.

Statistics tell me that Paoli was incorporated in 1930. The population was 55 when we left; it is 41 today. It covers just 0.3 square miles, all land, no water. The bank is gone, the school is gone, the pool hall has collapsed, the grocery is a jumbled pile of wood. A few houses look lived-in, including ours, but I've seen no people when I have driven through. I stopped at one house just to get in touch with someone, but no one was there.

The grain elevators are still working, and the train still passes. And Paoli has a Zip Code and a sign on the highway, so it still exists, officially, as well as in my memory.

LJW 03/06/09

COLORADO

See the clear blue skies
Mountains rise
Tears to my eyes
Realize I'm home.

Caressed by the soft cool air
Sweeter here than anywhere
No where else quite so fair
I know I'm home.

Gentle breezes wrap around me
Like a friendly warm embrace
Taking all my cares away
Putting a smile on my face.

Close my eyes and breathe
That sweet, sweet air once again
I know I'm home.

NOW AND THEN

On a calm quiet day
When all on my own
I read to myself
In a quiet tone

Some things I had written
That no one had heard
Accentuating so properly
Each separate word.

Pretending that I was
a rapt audience
Who couldn't care less
The readings made sense.

Forgive me my ego
Forgive me my pride
But just for an hour
I felt good inside.

Some things are forgotten
and lost in the past
But if I record them
Then maybe they'll last.

People and places
An idea, a wish,
A glorious feeling,
A sunset, a fish.

A special encounter
A casual glance
is all that is needed
to make my heart dance.

LJW 4/21/2008

LADIES OF THE MOUNTAINS

They stand serenely on the slopes
In their loveliest gowns
Jewels glittering in their hair
Like belles on the ballroom stairs
Awaiting their escorts.

Tall, trim, graceful
With smooth pale skin,
They sway gently
To music only they can hear.
They stand in soft low grasses
Among buttercups and lupine
And tiny purple asters.

Gathering gossip from each breeze,
They pass it on in low voices,
They never shout or grumble.
They keep their elbows to themselves
And seldom mingle with their neighbors.

But when the first chill winds of winter blow
They don glittering, golden costumes,
Twirling, sweeping, bowing, dancing,
Tossing their heads.
Shocking the stoic mountain.

Until, exhausted at the effort,
They let the gold drop at their feet
And sigh into slumber
Until spring.

If I had a daughter
I would call her Aspen.

IF LOVE WERE BEANS

If love were beans
I'd have a pile
Of every color, large and small,
To sift between my fingers
While feeling memories softly fall.

If love were scented oil
I'd have enough
Within my hands
To softly coat my neck and shoulders
And caress my throat.

If love were tears
My eyes would gleam
At every thought of sweet romance
To make the lonely hours seem
Just a melancholy dance.

If love were gold
I'd have a chest
Of pirate's treasure gleaming bright
To put my troubled thoughts at rest
When coming darkly in the night

Love can be red
And flashing light
Piercing hearts with tender pain
That drags us sleepless through the night
To face the torment once again.

But love is smoke
That takes our breath away
And blinds our eyes and then is flown
Denying every beauty
But its own.

If love were gone
And life were bleak
As heavy winter every day,
To whom would my bereft heart speak
If you and love should go away?

LJW 3/1/99

A YEAR AGO

A year ago today the sun shone dim
The birds were silent
Remembering him.

The space he left, so large and still
Has memories and dreams
Enough to fill

He stands behind me as I write
His presence adding
Brighter light

His hands upon my shoulders rest
Light as lace
Warm and blest

Don't count the time, he seems to say,
I haven't gone
Too far away

One day when you pass through that door
We'll be together
Evermore.

Sweet dreams, my dear, he whispered low
Calm your fears
Now I must go.

SECOND LOVE

How do you know it's love?
It's not so different from the first;
One is heady wine, the other
Fine champagne.
Does aged wood burn faster, easier?
You've been there before, you know
The signs and where they lead.
The first was an explosion.
The second like the rising sun;
One sparks, the other glows.
True love is not frivolous but warm,
Comfortable in its excitement.
The first was a whirlwind
The last like a warm breeze in fall.
The first had a future;
Now, the future is today
And time must not be wasted.
When one flame cools
While another heats up,
At which
Shall I warm my heart?

ALWAYS WITH ME

I've memorized your smile
The way it bends a little to the right,
The way it comes and goes like birds in flight,
I never will forget your smile.

I've memorized your eyes.
Their gentle blueness as they catch the light,
The way they fill my heart with warm delight,
I'll never lose those shining eyes.

The way you move,
Your voice, your laugh,
Are with me everywhere.

Your hands, your arms,
The way you feel,
Your touch is always there.

I've memorized your voice,
The soft inflection when you call my name,
No matter when or where, it's just the same,
I'll always hear your laughing voice.

I've memorized your style,
I'd know you at a glance a mile away,
You could be in Paree or Mandalay,
I'd know you by your noble style.

Though you are gone,
You'll still be here
A vital part of me.

No place too far,
No time too long,
To dim my memory.

SWINGING

I am swinging in the hammock of love,
touching neither earth nor clouds above,

Suspended in a world of aching doubt,
Wanting to scream but daring not to shout.

May I never tumble through sweetly scented air,
Knowing it can only lead
Nowhere.

FOR A WHILE

I sit in the chair where you often sit
Feeling your warmth and the beat of your heart
Sensing your voice even though we're apart
For a while.

I silently speak to your memory,
Which rests on the top of my mind all day,
And I hear the answer that you would say
With a smile.

Then the loneliness creeps in once again
And I ache for the boundless joy you bring
And I long once more for my heart to sing
Like a child.

Will you come again, will I feel your touch
Will the world shine brightly once more for me
Will you bring the desire that will ever be
In your style.

Reality ends when you're out of sight
The world hangs suspended 'til loss of light
Then visions of you fill the endless night
For a while.

When you come to stay then the pain can end
Then my aching heart can finally mend
And my spirit glow in the love you send
Forever.

DAY AND NIGHT

Delight in days, what they may bring,
The leaves of fall,
The birds of spring,
The snows of winter, glistening,
They all give reason we should sing.

And if the evening comes too soon,
Take joy in the lover's moon
That brightens every yearning heart
Be they together or apart.

12/12/01

ANGEL

I am sending my favorite angel to you.
(I have several standing by).
You will know she is there when
You feel cool and relaxed.
She will come when you need her most
To wave her wings
To comfort and refresh you.
Her name is Lonair.

Don't tch tch and roll your eyes.
She is real.
Many times, when I was overwhelmed
By events or fears or regrets,
She appeared to me
In the night.
I felt her arm around me,
I heard her soft voice
And I slept at last.

Maybe you have your own
Favorite angel,
But one more will just
Add more peace to your heart.
Can we have too much love
And tender caring?
I think not.

She will return to me
When you no longer need her.
Sleep easy and be well.

ROUGH ROADS

The road gets rougher
The farther we stray from our planned travelogue.
The pavement turns to gravel,
The gravel turns to bog,

And when we can't go back or forth
And none can pull us out
And struggle gets us deeper in
It does no good to shout

Then just relax and look around,
The sun is still above.
And for what it's worth my dear
You'll always have my love.

What we believe is what we find
The best of life is in our mind,
So let me share your thoughts and fears
Things unheard by other ears.

I know I cannot walk your path,
Can't change the dates,
Won't do the math,
But try to help me understand
I want to hold fast to your hand.

I'll share your burden happily
And you can do the same for me.

LJW 1/20/02

FANTASY

Are you my private fantasy
Or something meant for everyone
Who needs and seeks the ecstasy
Felt only when that search is done?

Elusive is its name.

We never find it, it finds us
And leaves us wondering what is wrong
When every ordinary sound
Seems like an undiscovered song.

Whoever can we blame?

Should we embrace it as a friend
And take it tenderly to heart.
Hoping this could be the prize
We searched for from the very start?

Have we a rightful claim?

My life is charmed forevermore
Because that something dearly sought
Has changed the bleakness in my heart
To something that cannot be bought,
A bright enduring flame.

Whoever do I thank?

ONE

So here we are, you and I,
The blade of grass, the eagle's eye,
The elephant, the drop of dew,
All the same as me and you.

We are the same, you and I,
Our loves, our fears, the song we sing,
The tiger's roar, the eagle's wing.
The elephant, the drop of dew,
All the same as me and you.

The harlot's laugh, the infant's cry,
The muffled shot, the bells that ring,
Ocean's deeps and stars that swing
In orbits seemingly unchanged,
In joyful hearts or minds deranged,

A lapse of seconds, a wayward sigh.

I DO NOT CRY

I do not cry
When people die
They have to go,
I know I know,
I love them
All I can
Before they go
Perhaps they loved me too
I'll never know.

I cry
When people leave
To go another place
Where I cannot
Hold their hand
Hear their voice
Touch their face
Share their sorrows
Or their joys

I cry for me
For I am hollow
I do not know
How I can follow
Down the days
That lie ahead
While I live on
Though feeling dead.

I do not know
When I'm alone
If in some place
I haven't known
Someone cries
For me.

LJW 10/6/01

MOONDREAMS

Bright golden orb rests on a bed
Of deep blue velvet overhead
Shedding borrowed solar light,
Crescendo in the silent night.

I watch it slipping through a cloud
And share my every dream aloud.
I pray, sweet moon do not beguile
Me of my dreams though infantile.

My trusted, treasured confidant,
I come, your humble mendicant,
To ask you, leave me less forlorn
As, monthly, we are both reborn.

LJW 8/20/02

TIME

Leaves fluttered softly
Light green
In the sunlight
Outside my window

Finches flitted
Singing their melodies
At the feeder

The window glowed
With the warmth
Of sun
And love

Every day
Was perfect
Each felt better
Than the last.

The day after
The last day
No finches sang
No warmth flowed

Leaves curled
Dry and dying
Falling slowly
To their end

We curled
Within ourselves
Lonely
For the warmth
For the love

Cruel memory
Replaces
Nothing.

LJW 10/12/01

I am not finished with you yet
So pay attention.

Here's the thing that needs
To be said right out loud:
Your life makes mine worthwhile
Your life supports mine
Your life gives mine Richness
And Meaning and Wonder
Your life keeps mine afloat
When it could drown
Your life brings mine
Back from the edge
Your life turns mine
From dismal to delight
From longing to laughter
From weary to wonderful
Even when we are apart.

You need to know
How important
Your life is,
Has been,
Will be, eternally.

I've told you
In so many ways
But you may think
It is a light and passing thing
Just an attraction
With a bit of excitement
Thrown in.
Oh no, not for me,

Words alone
Are too weak.
Too thin, too watery.
Because of you
I am filled
With a robust wine
Rich and warm.
Deep enough to last forever.
How did you do that?

Thank you. Thank you.

TIMELESS

Time has no boundaries
Where love
Is concerned

Like a spiral
It leads us   Nowhere
Nowhere
Nowhere
It sucks us
In
Then spins us
Out
Leaving us
Disconnected
Without meaning
substance
caring
For mortal needs

Time refuses
What we need most

More time.

Time races

Through happiness
Time stumbles
Through sorrow

Please
Time
Don't end my spring
Before I have
Drunk my fill
Of love and joy

Don't bring cold
Winter
Too quickly

Let gentle autumn
Fall softly
Until
I catch my breath

Until my feet
Feel
The earth
Supporting
The terrible weight
I must bear
Forevermore

When spring
Reappears

As it must

Can I ever

Again
Enjoy it
As before?

Time
Will not tell.

LJW 10/13/01

HAIKU

If the world should end
before I say I love you
It will still be true.

ONE HUNDRED DAYS

I thought it was November,
Then you came along
How could it be spring again?
How could I feel younger
While struggling with changes
Feeling time passing so fast
Missing old standards
Recalling former talents
Meeting new needs
Enjoying tenderness as
So long ago.
Time goes all directions
It spirals out of shape
Snatches us from complacency
Takes us to places unbidden
Uses us in new old ways
Then drops us at the wayside
Like it or not.
Spring will disappear soon
In an instant
Please,
Not until I have
Drunk my fill
Enough to last me until
September appears

Again
And, too soon,
November.
But please time, leave me
Memories
Warm and near
Not tattered or worn
Always fresh
Bright, clear
Forever.

TOUCH ME

Touch me
So I know I am loved.

Words are warm and wonderful
Looks can move my heart,
But a touch is electric,

A jump start when my rhythm
Slows to idle and I wonder
Who I am becoming.

Touch me
Remind me who I am,
Show me what I mean to you,
Give me reason to love myself
As I love you.

I cannot do this alone.

WAS IT YOU?

The climb had been so long and slow
Under heavy gray skies,
Until a sudden brightness
broke through
To dazzle my eyes.

Like cool water after a dry walk
Like violets sighted in a dark wood,
Like sweet music after sounds of war,
Like rest after a struggle,

Was it you?

A flash of color lit the dimness,
The sweet smell of blossoms
Replaced ash and smoke,
The ringing of bells
As on Sunday morning,

Was it you?

Like a child running to my arms,
Like a puppy nibbling my shoe,
Like a kitten nestling in my lap,
How I love the feel of you.

Like an unexpected gift,
Like moon glow on the night air,
Like a visit from a dear friend,
Your presence pleases me.

Like the sweet wail of a coyote
through a summer night,
Like the swirl of an eagle
In the sky above us,
Like the first bite
of a tart apple;

As the first drops of cool rain
On a steamy summer afternoon,
So sweet is the sight.
The taste,
The feel of you.

LJW

BASIC MATH

I'd love to sprawl across the bed
To fill the whole expanse
With arms and legs akimbo,
In my own exotic dance.

But that would leave no room to share
A cuddle and a coo,
So I'll divide my spacious bed
To multiply by two.

OUT OF HIDING

I can't believe you're standing here
With your endearing smile
As if you'd been here all along
The lonesome weary while,

When all my life I've looked for you
And you were never here,
Where have you been hiding
Oh, my dear?

I wandered through a maze of years
Confused and full of fear
With others so amusing
But who never brought me cheer,

And now, at this late moment
In our lives you do appear.
I'm glad you're out of hiding
Oh, my dear.

The sun went dim, the breeze turned cold
My ears heard just a roaring din
The very moment I was told
That I will not see you again.

The song you taught my heart to sing
Has turned to something sad and slow
The only message it can bring
Is just - don't go, oh please don't go!

I have so many things to say
I cannot let you go like this,
We need at least another day
To share a hug, perhaps a kiss?

To have just one more glass of wine
And talk of things we've seen and done.
Exchange some silly valentines
And laugh with friends beneath the sun.

To break the rules, a little bit.
To take a chance just now and then
But ah, the risk was so worth it.
If only you were here again

To share a hug, perhaps a kiss.
We need at least another day
I cannot let you go like this
I have so many things to say.

THE PRICE TOO DEAR

What do we do when we crave
Something
Only to find that we absolutely
Cannot have it
Without an incredibly
High price.

Where do we draw the line
When the price
Becomes tolerable?
Who has the right to decide.

LICKING THE BOWL

Licking the bowl
At the end of the day
Reveals so much
Quickly forgotten

The edge is only
The beginning,
The part I can do
With my finger,
Wiping it around
The top and as far
As my finger can reach,

Savoring the sweetness
Of the latest
Ingredients,
The final touch
Of a true creation.

I smile and squint
My eyes in delight
I work the taste
Around my mouth.
My tongue spreading
It from palate
To cheeks and over
My teeth.
I lick my lips with
A sigh of pleasure.

Deeper into the bowl
I need a spoon to reach
The thicker lower layers
Where the solids
The basics, the serious
Ingredients
Coat the bowl.

Not so sweet
Are these tastes
Nor so light.
My lips grip
The spoon
My tongue works
To slide the sticky
Stuff into my mouth
Which accepts it
With seriousness
And without smiling.

When did I add
These bitter herbs?
How did they
Become so sour?

How long have they
Waited for me
To taste them
Once again?

PART TWO

PART TWO

THERE CAME A DAY

There came a day of warming sun and cooling breeze,
A day for dreaming;
A day for soaring with the birds above the trees.
The water gleaming.

On such a day the world is bathed in golden glow.
No sign of gray;
On such a day we gather all we need to know
To find our way.

LOVELINESS OF DAWN

Sounds of morning float above the trees
Drawing the lacy coverlet of dawn across the world.
Chickadee melodies sweeten
The cackle of crows
The chirk of squirrels counterpoint
The soft moan of doves.
Narrow ribbons of sunlight unroll
Across the lawn
Measuring the playing field.

A young rabbit turns
As still as stone
In homage to the sun, then
Enters the garden
To breakfast on strawberries,
A box turtle, stretching to its longest reach,
Bites triangles
From a hanging tomato.

A doe steps from the woods
On her slender stilts
Toward the mulberry tree,
A red-bellied woodpecker provides
A drum roll.

What's done is gone,
All's new with dawn,
Its loveliness can break your heart

PETALS ON THE LAWN

Time and wind conspired
To decorate the lawn
With blossoms of most tender pink
From high upon the tabebuia tree.

They could have gone unnoticed
Facing skyward as they do
And won't let go until the time
Is right to set their beauty free.

We wake one day to find
The yard is strewn
With blossoms thick as rain
So everyone who passes by may see.

When lowly human worries
Make us waste our time on fuss.
And we cannot see Heaven,
Sometimes Heaven comes to us.

SAGEBRUSH COUNTRY

Sagebrush shares the stage
With mountain mahogany
And yucca

A coverlet
Stitched by deer tracks
Hemmed with silver creeks
Embroidered with lupine
And Indian paintbrush.

Trumpets of thunder,
Spears of lightning
Sighs of summer rain

The prairie's gentle strength,
Its sea-like swells
A steady foundation
For eternal needs

Security and comfort are here
like a grandfather
On whose lap we gather
Warmth and wisdom.

RIVERS

Some rivers live fast, short, violent lives,
Wildly beautiful.
They crash over all in their paths
Grabbing at the shore,
Gashing deeply into the earth,
Tearing away boundaries, creating chasms,
Changing everything they touch.
Eager to complete the cycle, they race to the ocean,
To begin again their frantic quest.

Others flow gently,
Slipping and sliding along their path,
Stroking the earth softly,
Tangling in grasses,
Embracing the fishes
Nourishing all creatures,
Smoothing stones,
Enjoying the trip,
Making it last,
Pleased with the impact of their passage.

Both are enjoyed and remembered
For their excitement
Or their serenity,
Giving us life,
Enriching our souls.

We move through our lives
like rivers,
Affecting everyone we touch
Gently or harshly,
Nothing is left unchanged.

AT THE WATER'S EDGE

At the water's edge
Where the blue heron strides
And the sky becomes one with the sea,

Where the tides push gently
Against the stones
Separating the water and me.

There I long to feel
The ocean's embrace,
To join that fertile world.

Where in endless depths
Without boundaries
My thoughts can be unfurled

Without resistance,
To flow away
Relieving my mind at last

Of the clouds that hang
So heavily
Over the troubled past

Like a cleansing bath
Erasing time
The sea will clean the slate

And clear my mind
So I can face
The future and my fate.

LJW

STONES

I wouldn't want to be a stone
They can't go anywhere alone,
They cannot see
They cannot wink
For all I know they cannot think.

I like them flat
I like them round
I like them snuggled in the ground

I like to toss them
In the lake
And see what kind of pools they make.

I like them green
I like them blue
I hate them when they're in my shoe.

Sometimes I take one home
To keep,
To look at
As I go to sleep.

I've loved rocks
Ever since my birth
Because without them
There's no earth.

THE WONDERFUL SEA

I went to the beach
To see the sea
And I waved at the waves
As they came to me.

The gulls were gliding
Overhead
Crying and begging
For bits of bread.

I ran barefoot
To step on bubbles
Left behind
In shining puddles.

A wonderful, magical
Place to be,
My face in the sun,
My feet in the sea.

The sea that touches
A far away land
Where there might be a girl
At the edge of the sand.

Gazing across
The mysterious sea.
Imagining someone here
Like me.

QUATRAIN

The wind comes off the ocean fast
With musty scent and hint of rain.
Reminding me of anger past
Thrown hard against the windowpane.

Lauraine J. Wagner

THE MAGPIE

The magpie is a handsome bird
Black and white and blue
His posture a proud and strutting style
His voice is best unheard.

He's friendly, cocky, curious
Invites himself to picnics.
Gobbles everything in sight
His motives make us furious.

His appeal grows even thinner
When he shows his greed
His churlishness gives him away.
He's just a crow who dressed for dinner.

DISCOVERY LAUNCH

Oct. 29, 1998
2pm EST
Cape Canaveral, FL

Ripping loose from Earth
Piercing, crackling flames
Force Spaceship Discovery
Through the atmosphere's fabric
Taking our hearts
On a breathtaking ride,
Expanding our vision beyond
Our ability to see,
Pulling breath from our lungs,
Stretching our minds
To understand,
To believe,
To know,
To remember, once again,
That we are in touch
With the universe.

SEASONS

Overnight
Sunny spring
Became icy fall
Not from days
On the wall
But from loss
Of something precious
That knows
No seasons,
But trembles
In the heart
Where lies all
That matters,
Where spring
Comes and goes
With love.

LJW 10/6/01

MOUNTAIN ONE

The mountain's face is pitted with shafts
Left by seekers both young and old
Who learned after staking their all
She doesn't easily give her gold.

Bits of silver and traces of gold,
Which the mountain for eons concealed,
Cost the fortunes and lives of many
When mere traces were all it would yield.

The tailings streak down from the holes in her side
Like tears on the face of a lover,
Who gave all she had to the suitor who came
Leaving scars that nothing can cover.

The tumbling framework of adits
Form abstract jagged designs
Turning once heady dreams
Of rich golden seams
Into fodder for photos and signs.

Some rusted narrow gauge track,
On which rolled the cars filled with ore,
Pulled by the stout patient burros,
Still waits for the riches it bore.

The screams of the mountain have softened,
But the wind through the adits still whines
For the long lost years of excitement
And a bit of the harvest still shines.

Oh, the hunger for riches still drives us
And the mountains have not yielded all
So the seekers still bore through the mountain
As they always will answer that call.

The sight tells the tale of the mountain,
Its place in man's struggle for gains,
What little they found
Locked in the ground
Is gone but the mountain remains.

LJW

FOR LOVE OF SNOW

How many snowflakes does it take
To cover the Rocky Mountains?
A million-gazillion said the 5-year-old
Stretching his arms wide.
And he is right.

How many to blanket
The great white pine outside my window
To my delight?
Oh, just seventy million, I guess, he said.
And he is right.

How many to send me after my boots
And him after his sled?
Probably only five hundred or so, he said.
And he is right

How many to make our eyes shine
And our hearts flutter
Hoping for more?
Just one!
he cried
And he is right.

LJW 12/12/07

RESURRECTION

One dead branch bends away from living trees,
Dividing the sky into jagged angles,
Insisting on its place in the scene.
Sunlight accents its top,
Shadows cool its undersides.
It moves slightly, tentatively, in the breeze
Having no leaves to catch the air
To help it flow with the suppleness it once knew.
With stiff, gray sharpness,
Tension,
Strength,
Stark among the green all around,
It gleams like a sword
Raised by a leader of legions.

LJW 3/1/00

THE TREE AND ME

I saw lovely, tall white birch,
Straight as the steeple on a church,
Its bark was peeling all around,
Some had fallen on the ground.

If I could wrap that bark around me
I'd know how it feels to be a tree.
A squirrel might crawl into my lap,
An owl might perch for his daily nap.

A swing could hang from my strongest branch
Where kids could play at every chance.
Families could picnic in my shade
On sandwiches and lemonade.

The wind could make me bend and sway
And maybe blow some leaves away.
I'd drink the raindrops from the skies
And feel the warmth of each sunrise.

I'd be contented just to be
A part of nature's family.

LJW 09/91

PART THREE

TIME

When words are longing
To be said,
Say them
Before another day
Becomes another night
And then
Becomes another day again
And time is gone.

Every day is a new life
Another chance
To reinvent
The person we would like
To be
Or wish that we had been.

Hold no regrets
Do not look back
The past no longer
Holds us fast
So we are free
To move ahead
Our hearts will lift
Like rising bread

Our senses fill
With gentle fragrance,
Spicy sweetness,
Peaceful hearts
While timeless music
Leads our dance
Into a world of love
So strong
That we will rise
Without a care
To show the world
Our perfect newness

RULES

Rules, rules, rules,
Made by fools, fools, fools,
Perched on stools,
Enforced by ghouls
With vicious tools
In hope of jewels.

CHRISTMAS IS AN ATTITUDE

We sing about White Christmas,
We picture boots and snow,
Snowmen with scarves and stocking caps
Everywhere we go.

We gather 'round the fireplace
With warming drinks in hand,
And sing of weather frightful
All across the land.

It's hard to find the spirit
While basking in the sand
In deserts or on coral isles
Until we understand

That palm trees sheltered Jesus,
Sand lay beneath his bed,
No snow, just stars shone on that place,
So the shepherds said.

So Christmas isn't weather,
And Christmas isn't song
But Christmas is an attitude
To carry all year long.

LJW 1998

HOUSEKEEPING

If God has made a perfect world
With nature's loving manicure,
Why do we have this constant urge
To rearrange the furniture?

A greater pattern rules all life
With constant reason and with rhyme.
Find lesser dragons we can slay
And other mountains we can climb.

All efforts to control our world
Will last for but a single breath
And by those actions we may only
Hasten causing needless death.

Let water flow where water will,
Let forests thrive and burn.
Enjoy moon and sun and tides,
That's all we need to learn.

BELIEVE THIS

Everything is fleeting,
Molecules in motion.

Hammer and nail
Collide without sound;
The table against which
You slam your hand,
The wall on which you beat
Your head,
The stairs you climb,
The lips you kiss,
The books you read,
All are constantly moving,
Changing.

Wind weaves straws
Through porous fenceposts,
Rain parts air like a curtain,
A breath moves mountains,
A thought sways planets.

Truth and lies,
Evil and purity,
Flow together
In steady rhythm.

We spin, whirl, gyrate, float,
Bumping together,
Flying apart,
Constantly rearranging.

Stay tuned.

LJW 09/21/99

BRIEF THOUGHTS

THE SHAPE OF LOVE

The shape of love
Fits into my hand
Like a sun-warmed stone.
I hold it close
Lest it fall and be lost
In the stream of regrets
That swirls around my feet

———

A SINGLE FINCH

A single finch
Attends the feeder
Chirping as she dines
On sunflower seed
Alone.

Is she thanking us
For the lunch
Or calling for company
To share the feast?

Like a prospector
Who has found
The mother lode,
She cannot keep it a secret.

————

SUN AND SNOW

The sun reveals our worst mistakes
They shine like polished gold,
While snow turns them to birthday cakes
But, oh, it is so cold.

SCRIBBLES III & IV & V & VI

Each day I hoped for something new
But found things all the same;
It seemed as if we filled the stands
And just replayed the game.

Then an angel whispered softly,
"Check your attitude,
You've completely missed the point,
The day itself is new"

———

Cowboys gallop into town
Sittin' on their saddles,

Canoers ride the river falls
Workin' on their paddles,

Old soldiers come in their RVs
To recreate their battles.

Why not?

———

The odds are 20 million to one
That I will win big money

The odds are 70/30 that
Tomorrow will be sunny.

But no amount of odds at all
Can make a war seem funny.

———

Sometimes I really need to know,
But no one's here to teach.

Sometimes I want a certain thing
That's too far out of reach.

Sometimes I lie awake all night
And dream about the beach.

And sometimes not

LIMERICKS

There was a young fellow named Flynn
Who filled his Jacuzzi with gin
When asked for a sip,
He said, "Take a dip,
You can dive for olives therein."

There once was a poetry writer
Whose verse just got lighter and lighter
'till one breezy day,
She floated away
And no one's been able to sight her.

Someday I'm gonna be older,
Then I can be wilder and bolder.
I'll dress as I please,
Sleep under the trees,
And carry a bird on my shoulder.

A fellow with plenty of cash
Came seeking a woman with flash,
Found one in Key West,
But when she undressed,
He was gone in a hundred mile dash.

A beautiful girl from Key West,
Well known for the way she was dressed,
Wore nothing but beads
'cause that's all she needs
To star in the Fantasy Fest.

If people can't live near a croc
Then maybe they ought to take stock
Of their own attitudes
And change latitudes
To a place with no nature to knock.

THE HAIRDRESSER AND THE SEA CAPTAIN

The salty sea captain stepped ashore,
His rolling gait across the docks
Led him straight to his favorite hairdresser's door
Where he ordered a shave
And a trim of his locks,
And the cuttings piled deep on the floor.

"This grungy old cap will have to go,"
She winked as she trimmed 'round his ear,
"'Cause the girls at the brothel, I happen to know,
Have a strict code of dress
And with that cap I fear
They won't even look at your dough."

The captain couldn't believe his ears,
His passion for that cap ran deep,
It was his companion for dozens of years,
So a choice must be made,
And it near made him weep,
But sweet Trixie would be left in tears.

The captain returned to what he loved best,
But his passion for fishing was failing,
So he joined a crew and faced a new test
As he rose to the challenge
Of something called sailing.
To what happened, l hereby attest:

We have to agree it was no small success,
But something of which he was proud.
it brought a warm feeling deep down in his chest
To hear the great cheer
That arose from the crowd
When they won the First Place
Award At the Race
Week 2000 here in Key West.

IN PASSION'S WAKE

The salty sea captain's mother,
While dreaming of something or other,
Cried out to her son,
"I fear I am done
Go, summon your fool of a brother.

"Great passion was part of my life,
But I never was any man's wife.
I suffered your birth
In a brothel in Perth,
I hope this news won't bring you strife."

The sea captain took to his bed
With his baseball cap still on his head.
He gave up the seas,
Moved to the Keys,
And became a hairdresser instead.

A storm sank the brother at sea,
But he turned up eventually.
Rolling in on the sand,
He clutched in his hand
Something no one expected to see:
The First Place Award
From Race Week 2000
In, where else but, dear old Key West.

ANTHEM

Brown roses bend their heavy heads
Surrendering to winter's chill,
Mourning loss of pinks and reds
In calm anticipation
Of certain spring that lies ahead.

Our lemon locks have paled to grays
Reward for countless cherished years,
And as we face the coming haze
Of promised sweet elation,
Can we believe what we have praised?

No tender fragrant blossoms we,
But flesh and soul of care and yearning,
Uncertain what rewards will be
Beyond our own creation,
What wonders will these dim eyes see?

But if we'll have no second spring,
If what we have is all and done,
And naught is ours but what we bring
In humble innovation,
Then make an anthem of the song we sing.

MY BOY

He walked tall, broad-shouldered
Thin, too thin,
His dark blonde hair
Curled below his collar,
The blue coveralls,
A good color
Hung loosely on him.

His gentle blue eyes were heavy
Tired, resigned,
Not quite defeated.
He sat gingerly
On the folding chair
Leaning forward
Elbows on the table.

He spoke quickly
In soft tones,
"I'll talk to Mr. Daly tomorrow,
Then things will get better
It won't be long now."

Despite his relaxed demeanor
The air was charged
Lightning flashed
Through my mind
I wanted to grasp him
In a warm, tight hug.
But I couldn't.

"Don't worry mom.
I'll keep in touch.
I love you."

ONE MAN'S EXCITEMENT

One man's excitement
Is another man's yawn,
One prefers sunset
Another loves dawn,
Some keep drinking
'Till the well is gone,
Some replenish
So life can go on.

Some sit under a banyan tree
And contemplate their toes,
Some will plant and nurture
To grow one perfect rose.

Some enjoy life, some endure,
Some sing out loud, some hum.
Some waiting their time to go,
Some waiting for God to come.

Life is a gift for us to use
In any manner we may choose.
Heaven has no need for rules,
Because in heaven there are no fools.

02/22/02

STRINGS IN STEAMBOAT

Like gnomes huddled under a great green mushroom,
The string quartet spins delicate threads
into the air,
To be captured by umbrellas,
wide straw hats
And eager ears across the lawn.

A bathing beauty,
Maybe two years old,
In a Pooh Bear swim suit,
Dances and twirls around the musicians
Chubby arms above her head,
Red curls bouncing,
Oblivious to her entranced audience.

Young boys sitting cross-legged on blankets,
Wave their hands in rhythm.
Grey heads nod back against folding chairs,
Smiling, their eyes closed,
Their fingers tapping.

Thin cirrus clouds slip quietly
Over the mountain,
Softening the brilliant blue sky
Above the botanical gardens,
As if attracted by the soaring strains,
Of Brahms, Mozart, Debussy, and Beethoven.

Even the flowers seem brighter
When showered with these beautiful sounds.

LJW

RODEO

Like a field plowed shallow
The rich earth of the arena is raked
To cradle the inevitable falls
As men pit themselves against beasts,
For the thrill of the crowd
And the winning of a buckle.

The aroma of barbecue and beans mingles
With the dust and the scent
Of nervous cowhands and sweating animals.
Recorded music pleads with mothers not to let
Their children become cowboys,
Then sings of the beauties of our
Home on The Range
While the American flag
Is prominently displayed.

Is it just another version of the eternal
Confrontation between man and animal,
Between man and the elements,
Between man and himself.
Or is it all about buckles?

From the moment the rider climbs the chute,
Settles onto the beast's back,
Grips the strap with one hand
And pulls his hat low with the other,
He becomes one with his nemesis.

His future rests with the wild-eyed animal
Made irate by confinement in the chute,
Tight strap around his groin,
Raking spurs.
Bent on throwing this weight from his back
With leaps, twists and gyrations
Unnatural to him;
Fear ignites the air;
The crowd waits breathlessly.

It's a short trip
From the animal's back to the ground.
The rider lands hard,
Trading one pain for another.
He rolls away from the horns of the bull,
The hooves of the horse,
He rises slowly from the turf,
Slaps his hat against his chaps, and waves
To a sympathetic, grateful, cheering throng.

It's those buckles that catch the eye.
Hard won badges of honor,
Engraved in silver,
Inlaid with gold,
Worn with pride
By lean, long-legged, Wrangler-clad men
Who took the jolts in their time,
And wear the buckles to prove it.

Hanging on the fence,
Beer in one hand,
Cigarette in the other,
Watching and feeling the pain,
They limp on bowed legs
And stiff backs,
Their sun-leathered faces
Topped by tall rumpled hats
Rolled on the sides where
Dirt stained, sweaty hands
Lifted them many times to the crowd
From center arena.

They had their turn, in their youth,
On the wide, flat back,
The wild horse's bony spine,
For those eight seconds
That meant success or failure,
Until the next time.

And there's always a next time
After broken bones heal,
Torn muscles mend,
Entry fees earned.

Who wins?
Man or beast?
Both? Neither?
Who wears the buckle?
Who walks away whole
To face another challenge?

Young boys in high-heeled boots
And tall hats,
Cling to the fence
Stretching hands to their heroes,
Reaching toward their own futures.

Like David without a slingshot,
A knight without armor,
A gladiator with no weapons,
Armed only with resolve,
Each man challenges his own dragons,
The drive for conquest lives on.

Same time, same place,
Next week.

The show never ends.

Lauraine J. Wagner

SWEET RICKY
WILL YOU REMEMBER?

Will your tiny ears remember
The songs I sang to you?

Will your wide blue eyes reflect
The many smiles shared by we two?

Will your toes recall
Our silly rhymes
And your fingers
Our counting games?

Will your lips reshape
The many ways
We fashioned silly names?

Will your tender tummy
Always feel the kisses I put there?

And will you feel my gentle strokes
Across your smoke-soft hair?

Will you look through
Other windows
And see the same bright sun?

Will your heart remember
The beat of mine
When we slept together as one?

Will time erase these precious things
As your memory gathers more?

Perhaps for you
But not for me.
They're mine
Forevermore.

———

Grandmom, Oct 10, 2001
Your 100th Day
Your last day with us.

SCULPTOR'S TOOLS

Never experiencing spring or fall
Like skipping grades in school,
Makes life and time seem as unreal
As reflections in a pool.

Without connections along the way
We are sculptors without a tool.

02/20/02

AS TIME GOES BY

You must remember this
A fish is still a fish
A lie is just a lie
The fundamental things apply
As time goes by

And when the guys go out
The gals all smile and shout
Today we're gonna fly,
No matter where we shop and dine
As time goes by.

Cruising the yard sales
Never out of date,
Hands full of plastic
We can hardly wait,
Give us the car
And open up that gate,
On us you can rely.

It's still the same old jargon,
Who got the greatest bargain?
"It's mine," we all will cry.

The world will always welcome shoppers
As time goes by.

GARDENING

My gardening's done
I hope they thrive,
Those tiny things I planted,
Impatiens in their tender bed
Encouragement incanted.

Some gentle words
In troubled ears
For those who need to hear them
Were planted, too, with fervent hope
That wisdom will endear them.

The first I water with a hose
The second with my tears
Hoping to dispel a host
Of worries and of fears.

11/20/01

NIGHT SONG

A mockingbird sings
Throughout the night beside my door.
She tells the world of those who cannot sleep
That love will come,
Be calm, be calm.

Leave open every door into your heart
For song to flow and move
And carry you upon its wings
Away from dim and tangled roots
That pull you back, insisting
The past be honored above all.

But let the song become your anthem
Rising from the cherished years,
Leave the past at peaceful rest

Soar into joy,
Face tomorrow's sun, drink its warmth
To nurture sweet desires renewed,
Giving life to myths and dreams
As real as moon
And mockingbird song.

AS LONG AS THE CHILDREN ARE DANCING

As long as the children are dancing
While the song of the flute fills the canyon
As long as the shadows give way to the morning
And gently the doves announce the new day,
And we smile.

As long as the fishes can struggle upstream
While antelope rest in the hollows
While thunder and lightning deliver their promise
And life-giving rain is what follows,
And we rest.

We look to the cloud-covered distance
And wonder what mysteries lie hidden,
Though every great peak leads but to another
Too far for our eyes to discern,
But the wind has discovered in her endless wanders
The wisdom we needed to learn:

To treasure the gifts we wake to each day,
Never doubt they are all that we need.
And to know that beyond the furthest peak
In vales full of beauty and sun
The children are dancing to music of flutes
And like us, they have only begun.

ALL I HAVE TO GIVE

Hello, what a pleasant surprise,
Come in, please.
I'm so glad you came.
Sit here by the window
Where you can see
The sun on the garden.
Lovely isn't it?

Would you like some grapes?
It's all I have to offer, I'm sorry.
I haven't shopped lately
And I haven't baked in ages.

Oh yes, I have time,
Nothing I would rather do.
I'll just put the kettle on
While you tell me what's new
With you.

Another cup of tea?
No? Must you go?
Oh yes, I see,
The garden is in shade now.
Has it been that long?

Don't apologize,
I enjoyed every minute.
I'm glad you're feeling better.

Isn't it wonderful
What grapes and tea can do?

www.ingramcontent.com/pod-product-compliance
Lightning Source LLC
Chambersburg PA
CBHW060321050426
42449CB00011B/2594